Joy
Begins
with You

Joy
Begins
with You

Donald McKinney

Nashville • Abingdon Press • New York

JOY BEGINS WITH YOU

Copyright © 1975 by Abingdon Press

Library of Congress Cataloging in Publication Data

MCKINNEY, DONALD, 1909-
    Joy begins with you.
    1. Joy—Meditations.   I. Title.
BV4832.2.M199   242   74-20523

ISBN 0-687-20647-2

To   Shirley Corder,
school secretary, whose radiant life
has brought joy into the hearts of children

Preface

YOU are the most important person in the world! You have touched the lives of other people. You have given them direction in life. You have inspired them. You have enriched their lives. There is a woman somewhere who remembers you because you were the manager of the store where she first found work out of high school. You helped her to make change, to greet customers in a friendly manner.

There is a man somewhere, maybe a great doctor, writer, musician, great because he sat in your classroom when you were a teacher. You believed in him and made him have faith that he could amount to something.

When you were a librarian in a small town you opened books of inspiration with colorful pictures to country boys and girls. Did you know that you were opening the windows of the world to them?

You were a mother or a father who taught a boy and a girl to be honest and to have faith, to believe in God, in the future, and in the United States of America.

At the gate of the Friends Fellowship Community in Richmond, Indiana, are wise words, "One does not grow old in years, he becomes old by not growing."

JOY BEGINS WITH YOU

So it is with all. The spirit of man is a living flame. You have lighted a candle in the lives of others that to them has become an eternal light inspiring men and women everywhere to reach for a star.

Donald McKinney

Contents

JOY BEGINS WITH YOU

How Beautiful
You Are

Ye are the light of the world. . . . Let your light so shine before men, that they may see your good works, and glorify your Father which is in heaven.

–Matthew 5:14–16

You may remember the old-time revival, once a must to the small country church. A strong, God-fearing preacher could usually pack the church with people from around the countryside who had not been in a church in years. With the evangelist usually came special music which was in itself a great attraction.

It was to one of these revivals and homecomings that I went one Sunday morning. The white frame church was nestled in a green valley with a river and a few houses surrounding it together with the steep, tree-covered hills.

Special music for the morning was provided by the Rainbow Singers, a trio of college students who talked and sang as they played their musical instruments. George Dooms, director of the Tri-State Youth for Christ, said, "The only thing about these young people that surpasses their talent is their love for Jesus Christ, and through him, for people."

When the morning service ended, the young musicians lined up at the entry to the church and 273 men, women, and children filed down the center aisle of the church to greet them. As I neared the front of the church I could hear such remarks as "you have a gift for music," "the Lord is with you," "I enjoyed your gospel message." There was much nodding, smiling, and handshaking—all so real in the lives of rural people.

11

Frances Wallar played the flute. She has a beautiful voice and sang solo. She gave a heartwarming testimony. She made her flute "talk." When I took her hand I said to her, "Has anyone told you today how beautiful you are?"

There are no words that can describe the glow that came onto her face. Of course no one had told her she was beautiful. She sought me out of the crowd during the dinner hour to talk before she and the other singers got into their automobile to drive back to college.

How long has it been since someone has told *you* that you are beautiful? Do you feel this way about yourself? You see, Frances Wallar knew she could sing. She knew she could play the flute. Hundreds of people told her this every day that she appeared before a church congregation. But, to be told that she was beautiful?

Let's talk about you. Do you know why you are beautiful in the eyes of other people? Maybe it is because you told a stranger how to find his way; maybe because you gave away a smile to a lonely person; or maybe because people know that no matter to whom you are talking you have something good to say about them. All of us reflect the goodness in our lives. We cannot hide our light under a bushel.

It is very unlikely that our paths will ever cross again, but I will never forget the glow that came into the eyes of Frances Wallar, nor will she ever forget that someone saw her as a beautiful woman, not just someone who can sing. And the gift did not cost the giver anything. The gift of ourselves is the most precious gift of all.

Jesus Christ lifted men. By his words he gave men faith to live again. Each one of us has this power to lift because we are the *children* of God.

Who Passed
You the Ball?

Freely ye have received, freely give.
—Matthew 10:8

A Christian bears a great responsibility in life not only to himself, but to others and to God. In a sense, our life throws a shadow into many places. People pattern their lives after us whether our lives are good or bad. Most people live good lives and strive to make them better each day. A father wants his son to pattern after him; a mother wants her daughter to pattern after her. Parents have a great deal of pride in the standards they set for their children. Is it not true that every one of us owes much to others who have helped us to become what we are?

I well remember the Sunday morning when Jimmie Greene's picture appeared on the sports page of the hometown paper. He had been the hero of the basketball game the Friday night before the Sunday paper came out. It was Jimmie Greene's keen eye for the basket that helped his team to win the sectional basketball tourney and go to the regional.

A seventeen-year-old boy plays hard for his school, but he is human and praise can go to his head. Jimmie was bragging a little too much in the locker room (Monday after his picture had appeared) about how his shot won the game by giving his team a one-point edge over a hard-fighting opponent, when the coach said to him:

"Who passed you the ball?"

13

Sometimes we need to ask ourselves this question. A boy goes to college, wins many honors, graduates to a fine job. A high school principal passed the ball by awarding the boy a paid scholarship without which he would never have gone to college.

A teacher says to a lonely child, "I believe in you." A storekeeper says to a clerk, "You treated that customer with great courtesy and honesty. I'm glad to have you as a member of my sales staff."

No matter how successful we are in life we are the product of many people who touched our lives and helped us along the way: our parents, our brothers and sisters, our Sunday school teachers, our public school teachers, our classmates, our fellow workers in every field we have been. We are constantly learning every day, constantly growing. We catch a ball, but we also pass it back. We take, but we give.

As a ten-year-old boy I sat in the Christian church Sunday school and looked at the hole in the sole of the shoe of my Sunday school teacher. I did not know that she was the wife of a poor farmer and did not have money to buy a pair of new shoes. I know now that it was more important to her to be there and teach that class of boys than it was to have good shoes.

Ada Kincaid taught me some values in life that were directly related to the Sunday school lessons. She was a rich woman in what she had to give to her boys, and she freely gave. She taught so well without saying a word that it is not where we live, how rich or talented we are that makes us stand out as people, but the importance is in giving to others what we have. My father illustrated this to me when I was a boy. I was riding with him on a wagon pulled by a big team of horses. The load of corn was heavy and the pin in the doubletree broke. The wagon stopped. I could not believe that so small a pin was a vital link to moving that load of corn. I could see the big wheels and the sturdy bed and tongue of the wagon. But who noticed a tiny pin?

Someone passes us the ball. Maybe it is just a little thing, but like the outcome of the basketball game, it can change our entire lives.

The Joy
of Being Alive

Sing unto him a new song; . . . the earth is full of the good-ness of the Lord.

—*Psalm 33:3–5*

Mrs. Perkins was ironing one morning when her neighbor came over to visit before washing her dishes. Seeing a pile of shirts and pants for a small boy, she said,

"Don't you get tired with all the washing and ironing you have to do for Freddie? Boys get so dirty."

"Oh, no," Mrs. Perkins replied as she brushed the hair out of her face and went on with her ironing. "I am so thankful I have a little boy to wash and iron for.

"Oh," she added, "I'm not trying to be a Pollyanna. You see I lost two children, both at three months, and the doctor said there was no use to try again. Freddie is so precious to me—the only child I'll ever have."

This is the only life we will ever have here on earth. We pass once and we are never coming back. Only one person came back—Jesus Christ. "I will come again," he said. And so we must go on to the kingdom that is eternal. So, how glad we ought to be to be alive and to grow and to dream.

How sorrowful life must be for him who awakens in the morning and thinks, "Gosh! Another day! Have to get up and dress and wash and get breakfast and go to work." Here is the attitude of a person who does not smell the green grass or hear the birds singing, does not say a prayer as he bites into buttered toast, does not feel

16

elated at the smell of frying bacon, cannot smile as he sees the face of a loved one, feels the dread of facing another day. What happened that blew out the flame in his soul? Where is the boy of yesterday who had such dreams of what he would become? How can one rekindle the joy of life once it has gone?

One woman tells us how she did it. We do not know her name. The Bible does not tell us. We only know that she had spent all her money on doctors who knew little in her day and that for years and years every day of her life had been filled with pain. But when she touched the hem of Christ's robe her illness left. She had faith after all the years that God cared about her.

Sometimes we become buried with the little things of life. The "good" son resented the honor and love and forgiveness showered upon his brother. It is doubtful that he understood his father when he was told "everything I have is yours." And he added, "Your brother was dead and now he lives again."

Sometimes life seems hard. We seem to pass beyond the point of no return. The flame of hope burns dim. Is there some magic power to lift us? Perhaps there is, closer than we may know. Perhaps it is to lift our eyes to the stars.

A tiny green plant knows that it must look up to live. Only man, of all the animals, buries his life in drunkenness and darkness when the stars go out of his life. But, as long as he lives, there is within his soul the hope that some miracle may come to pass.

It came to pass in the life of Mrs. Perkins. She kept within her heart the sorrow she had to bear alone, and then God said, "I give you a son. Love and cherish him." And she did.

Please Touch

And Jesus, moved with compassion, put forth his hand, and touched him.

—Mark 1:41

Today a lovely young woman of eighty-two years held my hand for twenty minutes as I sat by her bedside in the hospital. She had a broken hip. Of course I did not know that by the next morning her suffering would be over and the Heavenly Father would call her to be with a son who had died two years before and a husband who had been dead for twelve years. She would never be alone again. When I was ready to leave, I gently released my hand from hers and kissed her softly on the white forehead. She was so beautiful as her eyes turned up to me. I understood each word she was speaking although no sound came from between her lips.

As I left the hospital I pictured her when she was a young girl skipping with her dog across the fields. I saw her as a young wife and mother holding her only son close in her arms and nursing him at her breast. I think I understood what it meant to be alone.

If you have ever been in a hospital you can recall the loneliness of looking at four walls twenty-four hours a day. For more than forty years I have been walking up and down the halls in that hospital where I said good-bye to the woman. I knew that God's hand would replace mine.

God works in mysterious ways. What if I had not been

there to hold the hand of this beautiful woman? To die alone without love must be a terrible ordeal. It is the lot of a minister to bring quiet faith and confidence to patients and a meaningful love and courage through faith to those who will never go home.

We can be so grateful today for our modern hospitals that furnish a bed and meals and medicine for patients. We are very grateful for our excellent doctors and surgeons who work night and day to patch up bodies and to restore them.

But one necessary essential is lacking in the big hospital. The hospital administrations are determined that "thou shalt not touch a patient." Again and again nurses have said to me, "The administration frowns severely upon my putting my arm around a man to help him sit up in bed." "I am to send for an orderly if he needs a bath." "I must not become friendly with a patient."

I know what they mean. I once volunteered to work in a hospital with patients. But when I read the rules I sadly turned away. The guide rules stated: "Avoid intimacy with the patient. Avoid discussing anything with the patient, just a cheery hello. Remember the importance of objectivity in relationship to others." This meant patients, nurses, and doctors. Privacy is a sacred word in hospitals. We may come to the time when too much privacy becomes a kind of solitary confinement, the worst punishment we can give to a human being. Single rooms, dead-end halls take a patient away from people. Granted, one goes to a hospital to get well, yet a man or woman who has been daily surrounded by people in an office, store, school room, feels the loneliness of being helpless in a hospital.

The Holy Bible tells us again and again "He touched

them." And when Jesus touched a person, that person became whole. May God bless the good men and women who staff our hospitals, who work day after day with the suffering and the dying. How thankful we should be for them. But—please touch.

Rose Hamilton

He that humbleth himself shall be exalted.
—Luke 18:14

Rose Hamilton is the name of a large elementary school and of a woman who spent more than fifty years in the classroom. Rose Hamilton could be you. There are many Rose Hamiltons who live in this world.

I met her for the first time wearing boots walking through several inches of snow from a farm to her school in order that she might be in her botany classroom when school began.

She graduated from Indiana University near the beginning of the century and became a high school teacher in Abington, Indiana. She drove a horse and buggy to school, played games with the children at recess, skated on the river with them in winter, and became a friend beloved by all who came into her classroom.

In 1922 she went to a consolidated school which opened for the first time throwing "city dudes" and "country jakes" together. Leveling would come later. A few weeks after the school opened, Rose Hamilton asked her seventh-grade class, which she sponsored, if they would like a Halloween party? And how many would be willing to stay after school to help decorate?

Ron Hastings held up his hand. "Maybe I can. I have to ask my poppy and mommy first." The room was in an uproar because of what he said, the city dudes outnumbering the country jakes. Ron laid his head down on his desk and cried. He didn't want anybody to see his tears. He wished he could be a thousand miles away, walking with his dog along the river, any place but in school.

But a stillness settled over the room. Ron lifted his head and looked toward the teacher's desk. She was standing there. She hadn't said anything. She was looking out over the room. I saw the shame in the eyes of those who had laughed.

We all learned a great lesson that day—that we don't make fun of people who seem to be different from us. Different in background, homeland, customs, but alike in wanting to be accepted, in wanting to be loved, in wanting to share with others.

When Rose Hamilton retired she taught English to the Indians, and there she taught first graders how to speak and to know that they were loved. It must have been a wonderful day in her life when this modest, humble, loving teacher got aboard an airplane to fly back fourteen hundred miles to her hometown in Indiana to be present at the dedication of the Rose Hamilton Elementary School.

A former pupil who introduced her said, "Over these fifty states are men and women who sat in the classroom of Rose Hamilton during her more than fifty-five years of teaching. Because of her influence in their lives they have become leaders in keeping with the dream of the public school with education for all. Ladies and gentlemen, I present to you *my* teacher." This was a proud moment in my life too—for I spoke these words.

Rose Hamilton would never say that she taught botany, math, or English. She taught boys and girls. Yes, you may be a Rose Hamilton too. You are if you care and you love.

Are You
Rich or Poor?

But seek ye first the kingdom of God, and his righteousness, and all these things shall be added unto you.

—Matthew 6:33

A wonderful and wise Quaker woman by the name of Mary Mills tells the story of her daughter coming to her one evening with a question, "Mother, are we rich or poor?"

You are faced with values every day. One cannot escape a current TV ad that says when you've got your health you've got just about everything. We think of money as something that makes for riches. It will buy things. It will buy status—sometimes. Money causes people to change their manner of living. They may move to a bigger house, may join another church, may become members of a country club. But it takes more than money to be accepted. Nevertheless money does determine where you live, whether your children go to college, the clubs you belong to, where you spend your vacations, the kind of car you drive, the recreation you engage in—to name a few.

Can a man with money be poor? Sometimes he is. Can a man with little material possessions be rich? Sometimes he is. Parents want children to have a good education, to improve their life over that of the parents—a better job, more money.

One teen-ager speaks of her wealth. "My mother taught me to be honest under all circumstances. We

23

didn't have very nice furniture in our house when I was younger, but the house was filled with love. I always knew my mother and father loved me although I didn't always get the things I wanted, nor did I get to do all the things I wanted to do. My home was a place where I felt safe and secure." This is one of many comments written by seventeen-year-old students as part of a high school psychology assignment.

Each student wrote about his experience. Few knew how the lower or the upper class lived and what wealth or the lack of it meant—in dollars and cents, that is. In 1967 I put on my clergy collar, picked up my Bible, and left my hotel in Manhattan with nothing in my pocket but one subway token for transportation back. I walked down the lower East Side of New York. I entered the worst of the slums where I could see against the eastern skyline the high rise, modern apartments which I knew were surrounded by green grass and playgrounds, built by the city for the poor.

Someone said to me later, "Weren't you afraid?" Yes, I was afraid. When you are alone on a street where there are no automobiles, and you see a group of boys on a street corner up ahead staring at you, you want to turn around and go back. You think—will they pull out a knife or attack with their fists, or will they respect the clergy garb? You continue to walk, at least I did.

A police car comes around the corner, stops, and a fire hydrant is opened. The water gushes out and two hundred children pour out of the shabby brick apartments and run and sit in the gutter. A priest joins me. He points to the shouting youngsters, "I cannot call God 'Father' when I talk to them. Many would not understand. They have no fathers, or they only know him as someone who is drunk and beats them and their mother. It is difficult to give them faith in life. They have no future."

That evening, safe back in my hotel room, I thought of the things Mary Mills called riches, "love for one another, faith in God, a positive view of life, hope for the future, friends in time of need." And I thought too of the sky, the trees, the birds, the air we breathe; so much that is free. And I look up and say "thank You."

The Blue Vase

Judge not, and ye shall not be judged: condemn not, and ye shall not be condemned: forgive, and ye shall be forgiven.

—Luke 6:37

Fifty years ago school books were permitted to carry stories for children that spelled out moral values —strictly taboo today. No writer would dare present such a story to a publisher. A moral can be in a story, but it must be carefully hidden. The story is clear and the moral is clear about a little girl who needed a pair of shoes. The only shoes the girl had were worn out. Stones hurt her feet as she walked on soles with holes in them. Her mother, through careful saving, at last had the money to buy a pair of shoes, and she went shopping for shoes with her daughter.

"Mother," Alice cried, as she stopped before a show window, "look!"

In the window was a beautiful blue flower vase. Her mother explained she had only enough money for the shoes, but Alice begged. "I'll make the old shoes do. I can put cardboard inside. They will last me for a long time."

"Very well," her mother unwisely agreed.

The clerk took the vase from the window and carefully wrapped it, and Alice held it closely to her as she proudly walked away from the store. She could hardly wait to get home and go into the garden and gather a bunch of flowers to fill the blue vase.

How beautiful the blue vase of flowers looked on the

dining room table. A few days later the flowers withered and Alice carried the vase to the back yard and threw out the flowers. Suddenly she began to cry. The water in the vase had soaked loose the blue paint inside and the color was poured out leaving a clear glass vase.

The writer of course intended the reader to understand that all that glitters is not gold, that we should not be taken in by appearance. And of course it was clear that the purchase had been an unwise one. But it was not a complete loss. The vase still held water. A clear glass vase is beautiful.

People are sometimes like this. We put our faith in a person. They do something wrong and immediately we have nothing to do with them. We forget all the good in their lives. We permit one mistake to destroy them in our sight. Life can be cruel. We still live in a world where the wages of sin can well be death.

We may be attracted by a big house, a luxury car, a blond head, a Gothic church. But many times the plain and simple things of life are the richest we can find. There are plain people all around us. They never make the headlines, but they are the salt of the earth. The Thornton family down the street had lived in the neighborhood only a short time. Nobody paid much attention to them. They kept goats and had a big family. But when Mrs. Green was suddenly taken to the hospital for an emergency operation, one of the older Thornton girls came and knocked on the back door. "I've come to babysit with the children," she said simply. Everyone knew by the tone of her voice that it would be an insult to offer her pay. And Mrs. Thornton was at the back door about suppertime with two pies and a large dish of beef stew. Just plain people who knew when there was a need.

Beyond This Life

I am the resurrection, and the life: . . . whosoever liveth and believeth in me shall never die.

—John 11:25–26

Man has through the ages asked, "Where did I come from, why am I here, where am I going?" Only recently, in the last one hundred years has he unlocked part of the secret of birth, but death is still as much a mystery as ever. When it comes time for a man to die, a peacefulness settles over his mind. It may be a preparation of the soul to quietly leave this world and to step quietly into another world.

We are a miracle! We see the blue sky. We thrill with clear, moving water over brown pebbles. We see the colors of the rainbow streaking through the trees and hear the songs of the birds. We have the sunrise, the sunset, and the stars at night. We watch the woodchuck racing along a fence row and the graceful deer flowing over the farmer's fence.

God gives us eyes to see and ears to hear. We can tell how far away an object is. We possess the ability to see color, but our dog sees only black and white. We not only hear sound, but we can tell which direction it comes from and whether it is a train or a police car. We can smell bacon in the frosty morning air and the aroma of newly baked bread. We can hold an object in darkness and tell if it is hard or soft, sharp or dull, light or heavy, hot or cold, wet or dry. We can even tell what the object is. All this we know through the touch of our fingers. What a miracle. We see only the skin of our fingers, but our minds instantly tell us something about the object we hold. Is it of any wonder that someone wrote "How Great Thou Art"?

When you go to bed at night it is dark and you are alone. You cannot see anything. Yet we know there is a world out there. You see in your mind the place you work, your dog, your friends, your automobile. But all these are in your mind. You know that you are going to sleep, but you are not afraid although you know that you will no longer be conscious. If you did *not* awaken the next morning none of this preparation for sleep would be changed.

Men die like this. They go to sleep. But we who sleep to awaken the next day find that our bodies have lost their fatigue. We are refreshed, ready for another day. We see ourselves in a mirror. We are real for sure. We see people we love. We are alive in a beautiful world. No longer are these things only in our minds as we lie in a dark room at night.

Death is like this. The difference is that we awaken in another world. There we shall see people too that we know. It will be a beautiful world. It has to be. He who can make an earth like this can make a world eternal even more beautiful.

There need be no fear of dying. This is why those who are about to die are not afraid. They are sometimes unhappy. But the unhappiness is the feeling of the dying person of sorrow and heartache for those left behind. Heaven has no place for misery and pain and shaking legs. Going there is like going to sleep and awakening refreshed. An elderly man said to me once, "I don't want to live another year. When you become old and you are in pain your work is finished on this earth."

It is a fact that man and woman can make sperm and ova too small for the human eye to see. Put the two together and they carry all the inherited traits of what the child will be. If man can do this, God must truly be powerful and good.

The Gift
of Laughter

The Lord is my strength and my shield; my heart trusted in him, . . . therefore my heart greatly rejoiceth; and with my song will I praise him.

—Psalm 28:7

Sometimes when we are afraid, God helps us to laugh. Do you remember your first airplane ride? In the spring of 1947 I flew overseas in a new Constellation four-motor plane to London, stopping at Gander, Newfoundland, and Shannon, Ireland.

I was afraid to fly. The war had just ended and the great Cunard liners were booked to capacity two years ahead. I had to report to LaGuardia Airport four hours before flight time.

In front of me in line to check in baggage was a man who weighed two hundred forty pounds compared to my one hundred thirty-five pounds. He paid three hundred twenty-five dollars for his ticket, same as I did. But airlines don't charge by the "people" pound. I had to pay an extra twelve dollars for my twenty-one-pound typewriter.

With butterflies in one's stomach it is not pleasant to wait four hours for a flight. I kept watching the door hoping someone I knew would walk in and say, "Come on, I'll take you home." Nobody came.

Things began to happen which prove how important it is to have a sense of humor when life seems to stack up against us. The DC-4 was the standard overseas plane. But my plane, Flight 51, was a Constellation which flew only on Thursday. I seemed to remember that t!.e government had grounded this plane a short time before because two or three of them had caught fire in the air. So! I was to be a human guinea pig! (May I add that the Constellation was the finest queen that ever flew!)

Next I looked around the room and saw a big sign with the words, Get Your Last Meal Here. When I stopped trembling I walked over and read the fine print, Before Boarding Your Plane. When I got back to my seat a pretty girl in blue was passing out dog tags. "Put one on your typewriter, your top coat, yourself—so if we come down in the ocean we can collect all your belongings." I'm not sure she said this last in those exact words.

But it was important to save my luggage or baggage—I was never sure which it was. Only that morning I was sitting in the observation car of the *Spirit of St. Louis* speeding toward New York. I was talking to Dr. William Cullen Dennis, international lawyer and president of Earlham College. In Harrisburg the train was uncoupled and I dashed to the diner in time to see my car leaving the station. I was on the section soon to be sidetracked to Washington, D.C. A kind Harrisburg stationmaster put me on the Jeffersonian and in the lost and found department of the Pennsylvania station in New York I found all my luggage including my umbrella. For a while I thought I would be going to Europe with only a handkerchief in my pocket. (The explanation: the car porter was responsible for personal possessions of his passengers and he made delivery to the lost and found.)

God rode with me that next morning five miles high in the air and let me see a sunrise coming through the clouds below. And when we came down over green Ireland, he had delivered me to a new world. How great a miracle that man can fly. God made it so.

Joy Begins
With You

But the fruit of the Spirit is love, joy, peace, longsuffering, gentleness, goodness, faith.

—*Galatians 5:22*

Yes, it begins with you. Some of the greatest contributions have been made by men and women who began life in very lowly circumstances. Because of these contributions we have many comforts in life; these are material things. We also have a high code of Christian ethics toward our fellowmen.

Dr. George Scherer, churchman and longtime college professor of chemistry, once made this statement, "If you want joy and laughter in the world about you, begin with yourself."

This truth has been demonstrated wherever man lives. We talk much about the need for man to have faith in God. We need to talk more about having faith in ourselves. Often we sit on the sidelines of life, fail to involve ourselves, and miss the joy of feeling our value.

It was by accident that Carrie Holmes found a place for her loneliness and the opportunity to express her love. In November of 1971, her neighbor's house burned leaving two girls, one nine and the other thirteen, with no place to live. She offered to care for them in her home so they could continue in the neighborhood school. The father of the girls got a room and after about two weeks found a house and his daughters moved in with him.

Carrie Holmes had had her life disturbed. She had found an unknown joy in planning meals for two girls when they came home from school. Before, she had been satisfied with a bowl of soup for herself. She had brought down her sewing machine from the attic and sewed for the girls who had lost all their clothes in the fire except what they were wearing. She had taken them in her automobile to school affairs. In just two weeks her life had drastically changed.

One afternoon after the girls were gone she walked through the empty house. She looked into the four large unused bedrooms upstairs. An idea came to her. She went to the welfare department and asked about foster children. Her friends discouraged her, "At your age you don't want to be burdened with the responsibility of children."

Carrie Holmes was sixty-two. She had ample means, and she certainly had the strength and the time. And so—during the next ten years, more than one hundred children slept in her beds and ate at her table. Most of them called her "Grandma." She laughed and cried with them. She sat by their bedsides in illness. She proudly passed down the graduation line and shook their hands when they received their diplomas through the years. Every week she took from her mailbox letters from those who moved on. She sent six of her children to college. Two became doctors, one a nurse, two were teachers, and one became an attorney. When she lay dying at the age of eighty-three, the hospital was baffled by the thirty-some who came to the hospital to be with her and announced that Carrie Holmes was their mother.

The fire had been a blessing for this wonderful

woman. It gave her reason to live and it gave purpose to her life. There was always joy and laughter in her household because she made it so. She taught her "children" to be strong, to share, to find joy, and to look up and pray.

A Woman's Faith

Who can find a virtuous woman? for her price is far above rubies.

—Proverbs 31:10

Were there no women in the world there would be no stars in the sky. Woman has, from the beginning of time, been a force in man's achievement. She has been the power that has lifted man from the barbarian to a civilized being with a culture and a destiny still in the future. She built America!

Men came to seek their fortune in the early days in what was the land of the Indians. The rough wilderness, the danger, and the hardship were a real test of a man. But without women there could be no permanent society. And so, certain sea captains ran a ferry service between Europe and the new country. Their cargo was women. These women came from the streets, from the prisons, from large families, all seeking a better life. They knew they must marry when the ship docked, that they were needed as wives and mothers. For them there was real adventure, including the long journey on ship with its poor food, sickness, and even death.

A ship docked one August afternoon at a port in Virginia. The waterfront was crowded with wagons, horses, and some fine carriages. Men old and rich had come to choose the fairest of the cargo. Among the women was twenty-year-old Mary Ann King. She had a stately air about her and she was the fairest of all the women. Genteel old men in white wigs and lace cuffs waved their arms with flourish at velvet upholstered carriages—symbol of their wealth. It was an indication of the life awaiting any woman who accepted the owner.

After Mary Ann had turned down a dozen offers the captain of the ship grabbed her by the arm: "Listen, you with your high and mighty airs. I want my money for your passage. Take one of them while they are willing to buy. I'm a businessman. Now you git and take a husband."

Mary Ann tossed her pretty head and shook off the hand. "I'll get me a man. Just give me time." Then she saw a young and slender handsome man, well dressed, but not with a fine carriage, just a horse. He stood at the edge of the boisterous crowd. She made her way to his side.

"Why aren't you choosing a wife?"

"I cannot. I am poor."

"But you won't always be poor."

Just six words, but carrying with them a clear promise of what the two of them could do together. He bowed and took her hand. "I never expected a woman so beautiful to be my wife."

"Oh, but I can cook and sew and bear your children and be near to you when you need me."

Man educates himself, invents an electric light bulb, makes a TV set, performs open-heart surgery, builds a skyscraper, and travels into outer space. And always in the background, sometimes seen, sometimes unseen, there is a woman who is by his side when he faces failure, to believe in him, to love him, to urge him to try again.

Sometimes we cannot see the stars for the clouds. But the stars are there, even in the darkest night. And it is in the dark hours of a man's life that a woman reaches out and rekindles a dying flame and there is hope again, and faith. Without her man would still be a barbarian.

Helping
Along the Way

These things I command you, that ye love one another.
—John 15:17

Ellen Klemperer said one day, "The saddest word in the English language is 'unloved.'" We were walking down the steps of the administration building of the Richmond State Hospital. She was the mother of one of the girls in a psychology class which had toured the wards in the mental hospital.

In a mental hospital a patient is sometimes forgotten by relatives who cling to the belief that a patient there is a person to be ashamed of. The same relatives freely discuss a patient in a regular hospital for an operation.

You may be one of the many people in the world who does love the lonely and the neglected. Daily, men and women go to the Richmond State Hospital to put on programs for the patients. Gifts are collected communitywide for Christmas. Refreshments and music are provided on holidays and Sundays. You may be one of the good persons who drives a car to a ward on a Sunday afternoon and takes a patient for a ride through the countryside. Or you may be one of the people who gives clothing and personal items to patients. Because of people like you, love and joy and beauty are brought into the lives of those who live behind the walls. Because of you they do not walk alone.

People respond to love. For six years I worked as a

volunteer at the Richmond State Hospital. I taught classes in typing and shorthand. This was therapy for many of
them who would return to society and to jobs. Twenty-
four women, unkempt, unpressed, with pale faces came to
my first class. The next week and the next brought an
unbelievable change. They began to come to class with
permanents from the beauty shop, in pressed clothes,
even to painted fingernails. In reply to my question to
one of the women,

"Oh, you ought to know. You come here once a week
to help us. Outside of the attendants in white uniforms
you are the only person we see during the week. Some
of us mark off the days with a pencil until you come
back again. We look forward to your coming. You
see—the clothes you wear—you come from the outside,
a world we want to go back to. And you come because
you love us."

Bring tears to your eyes? It did to mine. How little we
give sometimes, a little that seems so big to others. I had
not mentioned the word "love." I hadn't given any
reason for coming. She added,

"You make us feel like we are people. The gentle way
you talk to us. You don't look at us as crazy people. You
treat us like—like the people you know."

How wise were the words of Ellen Klemperer. You see
them in the classroom, you see them walking the streets
alone at night stopping before shop windows, you see
them in the juvenile courts, you see them wherever you
go—people who hunger for love. How can we go to
sleep at night without knowing that on this day our
smile, our touch, our words, helped someone along the
way, and helped that someone to live again?

It Is Spring
and I Am Blind

I am come that they might have life, and that they might have it more abundantly.

—*John 10:10*

One of the most beautiful cities of the world, sometimes called the "Athens of the North," lies south of the Firth of Forth. It is Scotland's capital, Edinburgh. It is a city of monuments; a city of the preacher and reformer, John Knox; it is the city of Mary, Queen of Scots, of Holyrood Castle, the home of the Stuarts. One can feel the ghosts of Sir Walter Scott, Thomas de Quincey, and Robert Burns, whose writings have been an important part of our literature—as one walks the narrow streets of the old town in the twilight hours. Edinburgh is the home of the famous University of Edinburgh which has for four hundred years been a learning center of science, medicine, the arts, law, music, theology, drawing students from the United States and from nations all over the world.

As one walks down the famed Prince's Street one can meditate on the historical events that took place in the solemn, brooding Edinburgh Castle, once the royal home of Mary Queen of Scots, and of her son James, who became king of England. I walked along this famous street in the summer of 1947, and it was in the garden that I met a man, long to be remembered by many who met him there.

The gardens were alive with the musical song of birds

and the movement of them from tree to tree. The air was fragrant with the flowers. There was almost a mile of beauty ending with the great floral clock which faithfully recorded the time of day and always drew a crowd of people to watch and to enjoy the color of the flowers making up the huge clock.

Halfway through the garden I saw a man approaching. He was walking slowly, pushing a white cane before him. He stopped from time to time. His head nodded and he moved on. No one passed him without dropping a coin into his cup. He was in his own way a master of psychology because as I came close to him I read the words on the white sign he carried hanging by a string from his neck, It Is Spring and I Am Blind.

We sometimes feel that God has forgotten us. We see the blessings in the lives of others. We feel neglected. But God did not leave this man alone. He could touch the flowers. He could smell them. He could hear the music of the birds. He could feel the warm summer air. He could hear the laughter and the chatter of children. He could understand the goodwill of those who dropped coins into his cup.

To see is a wonderful gift from God. But we must not forget that God created beauty for us to see. Suppose the world were just black and white? Or suppose the grass and the leaves were orange instead of green? There is beauty in the flight of the gull as it picks up bread we throw to it from the deck of a ship. There is beauty in the smile of a child, in the formation of a cloud, in the rippling waters of a brook, in the eyes of a faithful dog, in the call of a crow.

Do not walk through life for one day, one hour without the awareness of the beauty around you. A warm, loving woman showed her minister through her flower garden one sunny afternoon. She knew the name of every flower, where it came from, the country it was native to, the color. She had memorized all this, the exact number of steps it took before bending over to pick a red or a white rose. She had learned all this before she lost her sight.

There is another kind of beauty—the beauty in the lives of people. Parents, children, neighbors, look for it in one another. Let today be spring, a new day, a new season, a new beginning of seeking beauty and love around you now.

I Don't Know
How to Pray

One of his disciples said unto him, Lord, teach us to pray.
—Luke 11:1

You remember the people who come to visit you when you are in a hospital. Sometimes a person feels helpless and useless lying day after day in a hospital. And because of this it is a joy and comfort to talk to people from your world outside. You know the people who come to see you make a special effort to do so because they love you. And you know there are some who cannot come. You read their cards over and over again. You know that you are not alone, that you are in their prayers.

During the time I was in the hospital with pneumonia a man and his wife called on me. When they stood up to go, the wife said; "I'd say a prayer for you, but I don't know how to pray. But I love you."

Not know how to pray? She said the greatest prayer that has ever been prayed. She cared about me just as Christ cared about people. Six months later I called at a funeral home. The woman who did not know how to pray had gone to meet her Master. She had loved others as well as me. She left behind a little silver smile that would forever be kept in a compartment of my heart. Death only takes the body. The spirit and the soul are eternal. What will you leave to the world when you are no longer here?

I DON'T KNOW HOW TO PRAY

I talked to a father in a hospital a few days ago. He told me his son had taken a flight all the way from California to come to him to examine him. He was so proud of this son who had become an excellent physician. You see this man will never really die. He will live in his son, and like you who read these words, it was the father who made it possible for a son to live on and administer good unto others.

Faye Russell was an alcoholic. As she slowly died she said to me; "I started out with a cocktail to be sociable. Now I am dying and I don't want to die so young. My greatest sorrow is not for myself but because of what I have done. I have served cocktails to friends who have come to my home. Now I keep wondering how I could have been a part in the poisoning of my friends. Always when I wake up my problem is still with me. Please —please tell every young boy and girl you meet not to take that first drink. I don't want to die so young."

Have we forgotten that there is a Man up there who cares about us? Have we forgotten that Jesus Christ asked us to pray when we have a need? Have we forgotten that God answers prayers? Have we forgotten that he gives us strength in time of need? Have we forgotten that he understands us in our weakness and our temptations? Turn to him today and learn to pray. For it is through prayer that we receive strength. It is through prayer that we come to understand ourselves better. It is through prayer that we build up courage. It is through prayer that we grow. Love for God is a strong factor in helping us to make the right choices in life. Try a little harder to find out from him the way to go.

O Beautiful
for Spacious Skies

In the beginning God created the heaven and the earth.
—Genesis 1:1

The Hudson River has sometimes been called the Rhine River valley of America. In the summer of 1964, I left Manhattan Island on board the *Alexander Hamilton*, the old sidewheeler that had plied the river so many years between New York and Albany carrying thousands of tourists from every state during those long years.

The Rhine River valley has castles and vineyards. The Hudson River valley does not. The Rhine is swift flowing and shallow. The Hudson is wide and deep. The Rhine empties into the North Sea, the Hudson into the Atlantic Ocean.

There is no land anywhere in the world that has more breathtaking beauty than the United States. Wise men in Congress, the state legislatures have made it so. Laws have preserved much of our nation's beauty so that the millions who take to our highways every summer may enjoy the beauty of this great nation which we call home.

But with the beauty of the land the United States has another priceless possession—its people. Our nation is a self-made nation. Men and women by the sweat of their brows worked and saved and planned to build a civilization for their children. Men in Congress and upon the battlefield fought to preserve the dream of a united nation with liberty and justice for all. The American dream has come true for millions upon millions, a life that is envied by the peoples of the world.

I recall riding on the *Spirit of St. Louis* to New York. Across from me were a woman and two boys, the boys eight and ten. I was fascinated by the suitcase on the floor which the woman opened from time to time. It was a Pandora's box loaded with playthings for boys. The mother was on her way to join her husband at Altoona, Pennsylvania. It was only a short time until I had a boy sitting on either side of me in my seat, and I was reading stories to them.

Who are these friendly people of our country? They are all around us. You meet them at state fairs, on airplanes, in church, at the seaside, on a tropical tour. Two of them came up to where I was standing by the rail of the *Alexander Hamilton*. "Are you a writer?" one woman asked, having seen me taking down notes.

And here is a lesson the traveler soon learns in the United States: I have never met a stranger. People away from home, if traveling alone, could be gone for two weeks and never speak to anyone but the taxi driver, the hotel clerk, and the store sales clerk. But people are not like this.

A man and his wife on the *Alexander Hamilton* were experts on the Hudson River valley history. It was like getting a conducted tour through this beautiful valley. I was their guest for dinner where fried chicken was served up to perfection.

The day ended all too soon, and I bid my host good-bye, to step down the gangplank and to be swallowed up in the masses of Manhattan. But vivid is the vision these many years later of our beautiful river valley, its history and people, and especially two people who took me in and opened the curtains on the history of the courageous people who settled the great valley and contributed so much to the history and growth of this nation.

She Is
Somebody's Mother

Therefore all things whatsoever ye would that men should do to you, do ye even so to them.

—Matthew 7:12

Yesterday I called on an elderly lady that I know. I put my arm around her shoulder. There wasn't very much of her—about ninety pounds and a will to live.

The tears came into her eyes and she sobbed, "Nobody ever comes to see me. I get so lonely."

When we are confronted like this we stumble around and try to calm a person. We say, "Most of your friends are gone now. There aren't too many people who know you. Those who do aren't able to drive cars. And your children—they don't live close. They are busy with their jobs and their families." And maybe you can calm the elderly some.

I remember reading in a church bulletin a couple of years ago that one gets many things by going to church. One of the "by-products": it is the only place that you can get hugged in front of everybody and people accept it.

An elderly person has in most cases held a child in his or her arms, wiped away the tears, given comfort and security. But who touches or holds an elderly person? Because they have become old does not mean they do not want to be loved.

Just a week ago I remember reading the list of hospital

patients and coming across the name of Mary Ann Brown. She had been a student in one of my classes years before. She put her arms around me and hugged me tightly. We seem to do this to show how we feel about people. I knew that she loved me, and she knew that I loved her. God does work miracles in our lives. Jesus Christ knew that the love of men for one another made up the stepping-stones to heaven.

Mary Ann is about thirty-five. Her children are still in school. She had a calling about a year ago to become a minister for God in the church. She had her Bible open on the bed when I walked into her hospital room. Her face was aglow. God had truly called her to preach.

Have you seen this glow sometimes in the eyes of a choir member? In your neighbor next door as she holds her child in her arms? In the eyes of a waitress when you treat her as a person rather than as a servant? Or in the eyes of a young woman and young man as they stand at the altar to be married?

Why, when we live in a world so colorful and so full of adventure, do we find life dull? Why do we get up in the morning dreading the tasks of the day? Where has our enthusiasm for life gone? Give God a chance. Work for him, love him, care for his people.

The simple pressure of my arm around the shoulder of an elderly little woman expressed to her by touch that she was not alone, that she was still loved.

The name "mother" brings back to each one of us a wealth of memories. We must all grow old, but there is no need for us to grow old alone and unloved. I re-member seeing an elderly man walking out of the church very slowly with his cane. A teen-aged girl hur-ried up, put her arm around his waist, and helped him down the steps. He said "Thank you," but I saw a tear running down each cheek. How grateful he was that a teen-aged girl took the time to help him safely down the steps.

She may live close to you—somebody's mother who needs a ride to the grocery store, who needs the snow swept from her walks, who needs someone to take her to church, who would enjoy being a dinner guest once or twice a month. She could be *your* mother.

A Salute
to All Teachers

Study to show thyself approved unto God, a workman that needeth not to be ashamed.

—II Timothy 2:15

A young American teacher was once approached by a former college friend who had been successful in the oil business and offered a job as manager of an oil distributorship. It was a key position in the company that carried some status and doubled the salary the teacher was being paid.

When he turned the job down his friend said, "You don't think the salary is enough?"

The teacher smiled into the eyes of his friend; "It is not the salary that is too small, it is the job." He touched his friend on the sleeve. "You may not understand, but I have a bigger job than you can offer me at any price."

"Yes, I do understand," his friend replied. "Most men would think of what they could buy if their salary were doubled. You are thinking of your job of guiding one hundred fifty youngsters into life every day. You don't think there are many who can take your place. I agree with you."

Do you know that every parent is a teacher? Do you know that one-third of the children in this nation grow up with only one parent? You are a teacher so vitally needed in the home today. Do you enjoy your work as parent and teacher? The most important work we can do today is to work with children, but many children are being cheated in their needs.

A SALUTE TO ALL TEACHERS

The Bible tells us a story in Acts: "then the disciples took him [Paul or Saul] by night and let him down by the wall in a basket" (9:25). This is the story of an escape by night from the city of Damascus, an escape from those who wanted to kill Saul.

There is a legend that goes like this: An old man was making a rope. He did not know that the rope he was making would be used to lower Saul from the wall. A boy who worked for the old man, an apprentice, said to his employer, "Why do we have to be so careful in making a big rope like this? We can put cheap material on the inside and no one will ever know it is there. And make more money!"

The old man replied, "But I will know that it is there. That is exactly what I cannot do. I must be proud of what I do. I demand a price for my work. I am a craftsman, proud."

The rope did not break when it was used to lower Saul over the wall. The rope-maker may have been engaged in a lowly trade, but he was proud, proud of his craftsmanship and of his honesty.

Take pride in the opportunity to love and rear your children. Take pride in your job, too, where you earn your living. A clothing store salesman once said to me, "I get tired of selling suits, but I have pride in helping customers pick out clothes that look nice on them and make them happy."

A dentist said, "I get tired of looking into people's mouths, but I have made many good friends and it is a good living."

An attorney said, "It turns me inside out sometimes to have to defend in court a lousy crook. I know he's guilty, but I have to try to set him free."

A housewife said, "I get tired of washing dishes and making beds, but I'd hate to see marriage done away with, and I'd hate not to have my kids to love."

Is your job a big one? It is the biggest job in the world if you repair my TV set, change the oil in my car, take out my appendix, make a comfortable chair for me to sit in after my day's work. If you are a coal miner or a bus driver I am glad to shake your hand. I salute you all.

A Few
Copper Pennies

The harvest truly is plenteous, but the labourers are few.
—Matthew 9:37

For a few copper pennies Jesus could have hired a man to wash the feet of his disciples. John tells us, "He riseth from supper, and laid aside his garments; and took a towel, and girded himself. After that he poureth water into a basin, and began to wash the disciples' feet, and to wipe them with the towel wherewith he was girded" (13:4-5).

It was common courtesy in those days to wash the feet of a traveler who had come over dusty roads because open sandals gave little protection from dust. To Christ, washing his disciples' feet as he did was not only a needed chore, but it expressed upon his part that no man stood above another, that all men were equal as children of God. This troubled the minds of the slaveholders of his day.

There are many opportunities for each one of us to offer service to others in a way that no one else can. In your childhood you felt a sense of pride in skipping down the road with a sack of cookies, or a jar of apple jelly, or other goodies your mother wanted an ill neighbor to have. Women of the church spent long hours remaking children's clothing, fixing baskets for needy families at Christmas, sometimes adopting a family for toys and needed home furnishings. Sometimes children were loaded into a school bus with toys and delivered them to some family that had need of love and care. The lessons of giving from one's own hands had so much more meaning than today when through our taxes, welfare, and community fund, money goes in a very impersonal way to help the deserving.

My mother set a good table when there were harvest hands. I remember seeing my father with tears in his eyes one hot July day. He had hired three men to help him make hay. It was dinner time. There were no women in the house since my mother was dead and my sisters married and gone.

"You boys wash up at the house and I'll take you down to the restaurant for dinner." That hurt his pride. The table had been set many times in our house for hired help. To a boy it was almost like Christmas because there were extras like pie and cake.

Just a few copper pennies. We are not going back to yesterday, but we can go down and speak to our new neighbors. Yesterday we needed our neighbor—handy place to borrow a cup of sugar or two eggs for a cake. A good place to pass time when lonely. A place to help out when a new baby was born. But today, it is in our car and away to the city. We don't depend on one another anymore. But we can. People do not really change inside. And there are new fields of need that have opened up. Perhaps you have already found the reward of being a Red Cross volunteer, a Gold Lady, working in a state hospital, a day nursery, the YMCA. Not only do you get a lift, but you endear yourself to others. To help place a child in a wheelchair and wheel that child down to therapy and back gives one a sense of being useful and needed.

A FEW COPPER PENNIES

To perform his work, Jesus had to take a towel and to kneel. Here we see the humility of his life, his love for us, and his willingness to serve. Some of us may be missing these joys because we by habit pull out our checkbook and hand it to someone, a check instead of ourselves. We miss the joy of personal contact. Mrs. Jones baked cookies every first Sunday of the month to send with the church committee to visit the village nursing home. The one Sunday she took the cookies herself and found a new dimension in her life—seeing for the first time the people who had been receiving her gift.

Giving Your Best

They did cast in of their abundance; but she of her want did cast in all that she had.

—Mark 12:44

I was impressed by a story of love I read a number of years ago. It was about a little maid at the inn the night Jesus Christ was born in a stable. Whether God touched her heart or whether she went to the stable out of curiosity I do not know. But she slipped away from her duties of pouring wine and serving food long enough to run across the light snow to the stable.

The eyes of the little maid widened with surprise as she looked through the crack in the stable door. She saw the animals looking over their mangers, the visitors in their fine robes, the priceless gifts at the feet of the manger where a newborn baby lay. The legend tells us that the maid began to cry because she had no money to buy a gift for the Christ child. But as her tears dropped on the snow they turned into the beautiful Christmas rose. She stooped and picked the flowers and laid them at the feet of the Son of God.

There is another message in this story that so often is missed. It was a lowly donkey that carried Mary to Bethlehem. He was there when Christ was born. He was not beautiful compared to other animals nor was he of great worth in money, but God used him and he was present when the greatest event on earth took place.

An Olympian runner who had spent his life in training knocked over a hurdle and was out of the race. When a human cry of regret went up from the bystanders, he said, "Do not pity me. I gave my best. Pity him who does not."

The little maid gave her tears, the donkey did what he could, the Olympian runner gave his best. What about each one of us? Jesus had great compassion for the fallen. "I came to save the lost," was his clarion call. He loved everybody. He said that those who had already found the kingdom in their hearts were already in heaven.

In our community, if we gave our best, the pews in our churches would be full. Do we keep the Sabbath day or do we cast our vote to close the churches? A supermarket manager was rebuffed because he offered a special discount for Sunday sales only. We want our children to have the finest in schooling. Is it enough to know arithmetic and spelling if we neglect moral training? Teachers try hard every day to take the place of the Sunday school and church in giving our youngsters some knowledge of moral values and instilling in them the importance of living each day accordingly.

As a teacher I never gave a failing mark to a child who did his best. Jesus sought out the lonely, the discouraged, the rejected, and gave them faith to live again. His gospel is a powerful force in changing the world. It was a little boy who put his arm in the leak in the dyke and saved his land. It was a mother who said to a child, "It is wrong to tell a lie." It was a father who said, "Son, we must not steal. You will have to take the knife back, but I will go with you because I love you." It was a twelve-year-old girl who flagged down a train after she discovered a broken rail which resulted in her saving many lives.

The little people of the world? God loved the little lowly donkey and the serving maid in the inn. God loves you. Be ready when he calls you to do his work. Then do your best. He asks no more.

I Shall See
His Face

Lo, I am with you alway, even unto the end of the world.
—Matthew 28:20

Florence Hoerner, more than forty years ago, wrote a poem that I have never forgotten. She read it in a class of creative writing taught by E. Merrill Root, one of America's leading poets. The story is about a little girl who wants to look at God when she prays because of the loving relationship between them. We want to look at people we love. But how often have we listened to a minister say, "Let us bow our heads in prayer"?

Does God want us to bow our heads when we pray? We can if we want to do so. When Jesus went away he told us that he would come again. To many of us he is not a Christ of history, but a living Christ in our midst. Yes, God is up there. All the world knows this.

You may have known many hours of pleasure and relaxation working with plants in your garden or in a greenhouse in winter. I was working one December afternoon in my greenhouse when I discovered a potted geranium which had fallen over. The stem of the geranium had made a forty-five-degree bend and was growing towards the light. What a miracle! Why did the plant not continue to grow straight out from the pot? What power causes a seed to sprout and grow up? How much faith a farmer must have when he plants a seed!

When I was a small boy my father took his pocket knife out and opened a grain of corn and showed to me the tiny plant with leaves and small roots ready to grow. God put the plant there, my father said. But man must work with God or it will not grow. Man must place the seed in the ground, and water and warmth is needed to make it grow.

The plants in my greenhouse are helpless children. I must feed their roots. I must water them. I must control the temperature. If I love them they flourish and I am said to have a green thumb. If I provide for their physical needs and withhold love from them they sicken and die. They are like children and like us as adults.

Sometimes men become lost in life because they refuse the love of God. They walk alone. No man can walk alone and be happy. He has to become involved with people. He has to put himself in a position where he is needed. Old folks die rapidly when they are no longer needed. Those who live to be a "ripe old age" have been cared for. You are old? Well, God can use a man or woman who has had a great deal of experience in living. Ask God what you can do. Florence Hoerner saw through the eyes of a child. There was wonderment there. There was trust.

Is God walking by your side? Do you feel his living presence? Look up into the glory of the heavens, past the flowers, the trees, to the stars. He made them all. His is the glory, the power, the kingdom forever.

One Stroke
of a Brush

Come unto me, all ye that labour and are heavy laden, and I will give you rest.

—Matthew 11:28

Have you ever stopped to think what that one quality is in your life that endears people to you? Find it, develop it, and you will have the key to happiness. You may wonder how a half-inch stroke of orange from the brush of an artist can change a picture. If you are searching today for a purpose in life perhaps you need only to look deep within your heart.

In the year of 1947 I visited a museum and art gallery in Brussels, Belgium. There were two pictures in an exhibit in identical frames, identical scenes with one exception—that of a stroke of orange. The pictures were dark—a stone house with a thatch roof barely visible. There was a gruesome storm raging. The trees were bent beneath the wind and sheets of water were falling. It was dark and forbidding and frightening. But in one of the pictures the artist had marked a window with light, a stroke of orange. In this picture there was *life*. And one knew that people lived in this house.

All of us walk from time to time through a stormy night. Sometimes we believe that day will never come. We cannot walk away from our burdens, our heartaches, our broken dreams. And then—someone touches our arm and says in a soft, kindly voice, "I understand." Two words and our hearts begin to heal. Someone cares. This is all we really wanted—someone to know, someone to share with. And we look up and we pray, "God, how did you know I needed help? I was in too much sorrow to ask you. I thought I was alone. I didn't know you cared." And God answered softly to your grateful heart, "My Son promised that I would never leave you. And so I sent someone to help bind up your wounds and start you on your way again."

Life is sometimes a rocky road. I happened to be in a high school gymnasium not long ago on the evening when the coach was selecting his first team squad. Forty-seven boys had worked their legs off for six weeks. Twelve of them would make the first team squad, twelve the reserve, and twenty-three would turn in their suits. Five boys knew they would make the team. It was quiet when the coach read from his list. He had called out eleven names. One was yet to be called. And then it was over. A dream ended—not to make the first team and the status that went with it, to be the little fellow on the second team. Remember?

I watched the eager looks on the faces of a group of boys as two captains chose sides for a game on a back city lot. There was pride in the eyes of the boys chosen first. And then I heard a captain say, "Well, I guess I'll have to take Jim. He's the only one left."

The newspaper praised the choir for its fine performance. I said "Thank you" to the young woman who played the piano for the choir. A young woman graduated with honors from college and went on to a brilliant career. I said "Thank you" to a mother who pounded a typewriter to put her daughter through college. A little girl left the hospital well and happy. I said "Thank you" to an unknown blood donor who gave her life. Call them little people if you will, but they are the artists who add the needed brush stroke to give life to another person.

I call them giants. They live in every town, down the narrow side streets, these people who share their lives that others may know beauty and hope and happiness. You live down one of these streets. Because of you someone has walked into a more abundant life. Thank you.

God Opens Doors

He leadeth me beside the still waters. He restoreth my soul.

—Psalm 23:2–3

Long after the Cunard liner, *Queen Elizabeth,* was built, the owners installed, at the cost of nearly $1,500,000, stabilizers. These stabilizers almost eliminated any roll in a moderately rough sea and reduced the roll by 75 percent in a rough sea.

When you were a child and hurt yourself it was always a comfort to be picked up by your mother and to be told that it wouldn't hurt much longer. She kissed you and hugged you because she loved you, and the hurt was soon gone because she seemed to share it with you.

God works like this in human life. He never promised there would be no pain, no sorrow, no tears, but he has promised to walk with us and to sustain us. For some the escape from problems is alcohol, for others suicide. Prayer has been the salvation of men for endless years. Faith in God is a stabilizer that helps us to live with our problems, often to solve them. Faith in God can open new doors and lead us from the valley of darkness into the light.

Raymond Hollingsworth retired after forty years in personnel work at a factory. His dream was to get away from people. He planned to fish and to hunt and to play golf. He spent his first summer fishing. He took a lunch of sandwiches and sought out some isolated river bank or lake. He made two hunting trips into Canada. He played golf with a friend. Then suddenly life grew flat. He began to see himself isolated from life. He was doing what he wanted to do for himself. He had crowded others out of his life and found that he was walking a dead-end street.

One late Sunday afternoon he was driving home on a lonely side road. He had caught no fish. He had fought mosquitoes all day. He was hungry. He was still fifty-four miles from home when his car heated up. A broken fan belt! He started to walk toward the highway some miles away. No car passed him, and an hour later he heard the ringing of a church bell. A white frame church came into view beyond the corner of the dusty road. He was tired. He brushed the hair back out of his face, crossed the church yard, and took a back seat in the church, not wanting people to see his clothes.

Raymond Hollingsworth found himself surrounded by people when the services were over. He enjoyed the attention he got. It made him feel good. It made him aware of what he had really been missing since retirement—people!

He was given a lift for another two miles to a truck stop on the highway where he purchased a fan belt and was taken back to his car by a member of the church. He did a lot of thinking during that fifty miles back home.

Within two weeks Raymond Hollingsworth had become a new man. He had changed his interests, and people recognized this. On Sunday afternoon he drove to the mental hospital to pick up patients for a Sunday afternoon ride in the country. He became a Scout master and looked forward to going with a group of boys on a canoe trip to the Canadian woods. He became a Red

Cross volunteer worker. He was a happy man. Now people needed him, depended upon him, loved him. The experience of working for others without pay was an extremely rewarding experience.

No, it is not a secret what God can do. He opens doors for us. He shows us the way. Sometimes we take the wrong turn in the road. Sometimes we wonder if we can ever find our way back to the right highway. He will lead us. Trust in him. The ringing of a church bell, a broken fan belt, changed the life of Raymond Hollingsworth. And God was there when he was needed.

Where Is Happiness?

Whosoever drinketh of the water that I shall give him shall never thirst.

—John 4:14

Someone has defined happiness as a sense of delight with the world in which we live. It may be had when one slips into an old sweater to take an evening walk. It may be the taste of warm biscuits on a cool October morning. It may be the cooling touch of fresh sheets on a bed; or it could be in standing over a hot air register in a long nightgown one late December evening. Happiness can be the thrill of flipping a switch and seeing a room lighted up, or the turning of a key and bringing the motor of our car to life for a ride through the countryside. Happiness can be the touch of a child's fingers in our hand. It may be the wagging of a puppy's tail because he is glad to see us and he loves us.

In today's paper there are twenty-two judgments against people who owe small loan companies. These are people who are trying to buy happiness with what they haven't got. True they need washing machines and car payment money. True we want families to have color TV, and doctors' bills paid. People borrow money because they sincerely believe they need things which money will buy. One man says he has never had title to an automobile. He buys a new car every three years, and the finance company pays off the old car and takes possession of the new one. An uncle who owned a

69

casket factory in Ohio once said, "I hire a man with an eighth-grade education, teach him what he needs to know in one day, and he wants to live in a house like mine and drive a car like mine." If people feel this way it is because it is the American dream.

The laboring man's child should have clothes just as nice as the rich man's child when going to school. This is what we want in America. The laboring man produces the wealth whether he has an eighth grade education or a college education. He wants a share in what he produces. We have gone a long way to bring our dream true. You cannot tell by looking at the cars in front of the church on Sunday or by looking at suits of clothes inside the church which is the doctor and which is the custodian of the high school. All men want dignity. The poor want good hospital care for their children, a chance for a college education for the children. We all want this in America. Give us time—the American dream is nearer than ever before.

Happiness means many things to many people. To some it may mean plenty of cans of beer and a TV program. To others it may mean a good book and a fireplace. Still to others it can mean a job one likes, good friends, a vacation once a year, inventing a new product, solving a health problem, falling in love, eating an ice cream cone, finding a four leaf clover, or drinking a glass of cool water. The smell of frying bacon, riding down a country road on a bicycle, singing in the church choir, the sound of warm milk coming from a cow and hitting the bucket, and the hum of bees on a sunny afternoon is happiness.

The simple things of life bring happiness to some people. How do you find your happiness? What would you be doing right now if you could do anything you wanted to do? The man who goes in debt wants a kind of happiness now which he is willing to pay for tomorrow. His idea of happiness may not be like yours or mine. We may be far off in waiting for tomorrow for our happiness and we may wait too late. Jesus gave us food for thought when he told the story of the lilies of the field. Look around you for the common, everyday things in life that are so warming to the heart.

You Are
One of Us

Thou shalt love thy neighbour as thyself.
—*Matthew 22:39*

There are some people that you never forget. Carolyn Eliason Gardner is one of these. I first met her nearly twenty years ago. She was an outstanding student in high school both as a scholar and in her participation in various school activities. When she was named queen of the Wayne County Fair one summer, selected from nearly fifty of the most beautiful and talented girls, those who knew Carolyn Gardner understood why she won the honor.

Personality is a vague quality in a person. It is everything that we are. When we were children we were eager to be chosen first on a team whether it was London Bridge or hide-and-go-seek. We planned and worked to get a part in the school play. We groomed ourselves to perfection to get the job over many competitors. All our lives we must compete with others. We want to be needed. We want to be appreciated. We want a reasonable amount of success. This is the nature which God puts into a person's life, the need to grow and to achieve.

A number of years ago Carolyn's graduating class held a ten-year reunion and invited as guests four teachers who had taught in the classroom when her class was in school. I heard a remark which she made that has never been forgotten. I am sure others who heard it thought as I did, "I wish I could be like her."

One of the invited teachers, in making farewells at the end of the reunion, said to Carolyn, "Thank you for inviting me. It is the first time I have been invited to a class reunion in fifteen years, and it has been such a joy to meet so many of you again. I'm very grateful."

"Oh, but you are one of us," Carolyn quickly replied. And she implied that how could the class have a reunion without the teachers who had taught them, worked with them on class activities? This remark of Carolyn's tells something of the reason so many love her. Carolyn has had her share and more of sorrow and tragedy. But the glow in her life is eternal. Yes, you can be like her. It is no secret. She cares about other people. When we care about others we bring light into our own lives. It is as simple as that.

To be included is to be loved. To be loved is to be happy. Someone has said that the more one loves the more he becomes capable of loving. Another person has said that love is one of the few things in life that we can best keep by giving it away.

A middle-aged woman played with perfection at a wedding I attended recently. I commented about it to her at the end of the wedding. "Oh, Alice and I were schoolmates together when we were in the third grade. That was thirty-five years ago and I hadn't seen her since until today. She got so busy being a teacher that she never got around to getting married until now. But when she decided to get married she wanted me to play." One could feel the sense of pride in her voice —that of being wanted after all those years.

Carolyn is one of these people. Once having known her you never forget her. "You are one of us," is the only speech remembered from that reunion. How true it is that the little things you say to others each day of your life are so important.

Love's Miracles

He that loseth his life for my sake shall find it.
—Matthew 10:39

You have some person in the back of your mind, perhaps many names come to you, of people who have been a guiding influence in helping you to become what you are. These people can be parents, teachers, ministers, friends you have met on your journey through life.

One of the great problems that man must cope with is that of putting others before himself. "He that loses his life shall save it." Sometimes it takes many years to understand these words. But the people who have helped us are the people who have loved us during precious moments which we touch and then go on.

Peter Goulding in his book *The Young Minister* expresses the truth that we cannot understand people until we know them as they really are, their heartbreaking sorrows, and their struggles. We have to know their failures and the burdens they bear and their dreams. And this is our problem in helping people—we very seldom drop our masks.

The minister sometimes steps behind this mask and then he is beloved because the human heart cries out to share with someone—someone who can be trusted to keep only to himself the shared concern. I have often visited in the hospital and many times anxious friends have asked, "What kind of an operation did she have?"

Of course there is only one answer, "She will tell you if she wants you to know."

A pastor does his best work when he sits down with a family, perhaps an unmarried high school girl who is pregnant, a teen-aged boy caught on a joy ride in a stolen car, a divorce case pending. We see him in the pulpit, but the sermon is a minor part of his service to mankind. You ought to love that man because he sheds his tears with your sorrow. He knows what human suffering is.

But you—you can be like him too. We are all ministers. You need only to love people, to show your interest in them, and you too can help the unfortunate with their struggles, their burdens. When we care, God opens doors for us. When Alice Commons loaned her formal dress to Ruth Ann King for her graduation she was asked why. "Because I love you." And she added, "I know how important it is to look one's best on this grand night."

Ruth Ann moved away after graduation and many years passed by. It was twenty-five years later she read in the hometown paper that came to her that Alice Commons Harris had been brought home from a clinic to die. The next day there was a knock at the door of the Harris home, and Mr. Harris opened the door to a woman he did not know. She was carrying a suitcase. "I am a registered nurse," she said. "I have come to take care of your wife."

Words cannot describe the meeting of Ruth Ann and Alice as Ruth Ann crossed the room and embraced the woman lying upon the bed. "Do you remember me," she said quietly. "I am the girl you loaned your formal to, and you told me I would be the prettiest girl there.

How did you know that my father could not afford to buy me a formal for my graduation? I have remembered you every day of my life."

Love does perform miracles. The kind of a miracle that causes the men of medicine to shake their heads. Alice did not die. Ruth Ann cared for her night and day, fed her, bathed her, touched her, prayed for her. Six weeks later Alice walked across her bedroom for the first time. It was a tearful, yet joyful farewell when the little nurse walked out the front door. She looked back once to a husband and a wife and two children who waved from the doorway. She had refused to take one penny for her work.

"It's my gift to God and to you," she had simply said. "Because you said to a lonely girl once and now I say it to you. I'm grateful to God I could care for you because, you see, I love you."

Parting Is
Not Forever

I am the bread of life, he that cometh to me shall never hunger; and he that believeth on me shall never thirst.

—John 6:35

In August of 1947, sixty-eight young men and women, most of them teachers from China, Norway, Germany, Denmark, England, and eleven other countries, said good-bye. We put our arms around one another and kissed one another good-bye, and we said, "We'll see you again someday." And then we turned and walked away, to the train, the airplane, the ocean liner. We went back to serve in our own communities. We knew that we would never meet again. Parting is sad when you have lived and studied and eaten and played together for seventeen weeks. I took a sorrowful look at the empty tennis court where there had been so much laughter and fun in the late afternoon when college classes were over.

Whenever we say hello to someone we must always say good-bye. This is a truth of life. The Quakers believe that the word "church" stands for people, not a building. God has given to us in friends the richest treasure on earth.

As I write these words I think of a brother who lives three thousand miles away. He is in a retirement home. I have seen him only two or three times for a few hours the past twenty years. But I remember so well the gusto of his childhood—a bicycle rider, a pole vaulter in high school, a horse and buggy going down the drive with him holding the lines on his way to see his girl, of the nights when my mother walked up and down the road hearing the noise of battle in France and praying that he would not die, of a thousand and one memories. So it is with those we love.

A thirty-eight-year-old doctor flew to a hospital three thousand miles away to be beside his father who lay dying. They didn't see each other often, but when I stood at the foot of the dying man's bed and saw the glance that passed between him and his son I understood the bond between them, the contentment in the father's heart that he had played a part in giving his son a medical education and that his son had come to be with him.

Rodgers and Hammerstein express life in a deep and warm manner in "The Song of Love Is a Sad Song." So it is. The ball always ends for a girl. She tucks her gown tenderly away in a drawer. She thinks in the solitude of her room, "His hands have touched this gown. Perhaps they never will again. But he will always be a part of me. We laughed and danced and were happy. He said good-bye at the door—it was only minutes ago. Will I ever see him again? I can still feel his arm around my shoulder and see him smiling down at me as we danced our last dance to the orchestra softly playing 'Goodnight, Sweetheart.'"

Those of us who can cry so deeply do so because we love so deeply. God gives to us friends who give meaning to our lives. A father gives his daughter away in marriage. A man or woman retires. But God opens windows for us. We never need to say good-bye to memories, and we never need to say good-bye to God. He is our heavenly father. We will all meet again someday in a land where there will be no parting. It was Jesus Christ, the Son of God who said, "He that believeth in me though he were dead, yet shall he live. And whosoever liveth and believeth in me shall never die." Someday we will gather for a great reunion and those we have known and loved will be there. And there will be no more parting and no more tears. You see, God is lonely too, and it will be a joy in his life when at last we walk into his presence and come to understand the full meaning of the words of Jesus, "Ye are the children of God." We have wandered the earth, but we will some-day go home.

A Pair
of Boots

Who am I, that I should go unto Pharaoh, and that I should bring forth the children of Israel out of Egypt?

—*Exodus 3:11*

One of the great leaders and inspiring speakers of this generation was A. Ward Applegate. He was a world traveler, teacher, Christian minister, and extraordinary right hand of God. He devoted his life to bringing hope, inspiration, and love to the needy.

He shared this story of his early marriage: He was very poor, living on a rented farm with his wife, never more than a step ahead of the wolf at the door. Many of you remember the days of your life when you were never quite sure where your next meal was coming from.

Ward's father and mother were elderly and comfortable and godly. Ward told the story of a muddy spring on the farm and his need for a pair of boots. Sometimes he had to wade more than ankle deep to care for his livestock. His parents visited the farm from time to time. One rather miserable day the family was sitting around the wood cook-stove in the kitchen, the only heated room in the house, when Ward's mother said, "Son, your father and I pray for you every night. We pray that God will spare you from catching a cold and pneumonia from getting your feet wet."

This was a prayer of kindly concern for her son. I can just imagine her prayer going something like this: "Dear God, please take care of my boy. I know he has to wade

81

through the mud in the barnyard to care for his stock night and morning. Take care of him and I will bless thy name."

A few days later, Ward's folks drove in the muddy lane, hitched the horse, and took in a package. Ward took the package, opened it, and held up a pair of rubber boots. He embraced his mother and shook his father's hand for the unexpected gift of boots. Ward's mother quickly gave an explanation for the gift.

"The Lord talked back to me the night before last. He asked why I didn't stop asking him to keep thee from getting sick. He said, 'Why don't you go out and help him? Buy thy son a pair of boots.'"

Sometimes God speaks to us, and the solution to our problem is so very simple. That is, if we listen. But sometimes too we say, "Who me? You talking to me, God? Not me, Lord. Send somebody else, but don't ask me to go." But he does ask us. Jesus almost always asked a man to do something before healing took place, whether it was a change of heart or a physical action. How proud we ought to be when God needs us.

Has God ever spoken to you like he did to Ward Applegate's mother? Has he ever called you? Did you ever take a child into your home, nurse a neighbor who was ill, go to a mission field to work, give a sandwich or a glass of milk to a beggar, take a child to a store and buy him a needed pair of shoes, take an elderly neighbor to the doctor's or to the grocery store, teach a Sunday school class, make a telephone call to a shut-in, serve on a school board, shovel snow from the walk for an elderly couple, put out feed for birds?

If you have, then in a sense you have bought "a pair of boots."

Some Things
to Remember

Suffer the little children to come unto me, and forbid them not: for of such is the kingdom of God.

—Mark 10:14

Some of you will remember in your childhood how you slept in that cold bedroom upstairs, the big base burner in the sitting room. You will remember your father getting up early, starting the fire, calling you, and how you raced down the steps in a long flannel nightgown to your clothes that had been left on chair backs when you had undressed the night before. Sometimes you laughed and chattered, and sometimes you cried to your mother in dismay when you found the sleeves and legs of your clothes tied in knots.

But the resentment was a passing mood as you smelled the aroma of fresh pan sausage, soda biscuits fresh from the oven, and the coffee. You liked the smell of coffee although your mother would not allow you to drink it.

Maybe you had an old-fashioned mother. You wore long underwear that reached from the ankles to the wrists. After a washing or two the bottom of the legs were so stretched you could easily have put your head into them. That caused trouble, especially with my sister.

My sister was eleven years old and in the sixth grade. She had to wrap the loose legs around her ankles in order to pull up the long, black-ribbed stockings she

83

wore. Of course this left a long ridge up the back of her leg. She came home one day with revolt in her heart, "Alice Davis wore underwear today that didn't have legs. Her stockings fitted her legs and she looked pretty." Revolt was a dangerous attitude to have around my mother. My sister wore long-legged underwear until spring came.

Then there was the first day of school when I wore my new farm shoes. Not one boy in school wore a pair of shoes. I took mine off and went barefooted all day. I told my mother the truth as soon as I got home before my sister had a chance to blab. My shoes stayed home on warm days. My mother seemed to understand boys.

I remember too, the one-room, white frame church that was beside the railroad track. It was lighted by kerosene lamps with reflectors. The church had two straight rows of benches and a very plain pulpit. My parents took me there every Sunday, hitching the horse and buggy to a tree in the church yard.

Life was hard on the farm. We had no tractor, no lights, no bathroom, no refrigerator, no radio. It was a gruesome walk in winter down the path back of the house to the little building that served as a part of a bathroom. The rest of the bathroom was in the kitchen in front of the wood-burning cookstove. Water was dipped out of the water tank on the back of the stove and dumped into a washtub. There were no curtains, and the entire family sat in the kitchen while baths were taken. My mother said you took a bath because you were dirty, not to put on a show. Somehow we never seemed to mind.

I was ready to leave for school one morning and it was very cold and my gloves were full of holes. My mother seemed to hesitate before giving me my dinner basket. Then, her mind made up, she marched into the bedroom and came out with the most beautiful black cuffs with white palm gloves I had ever seen. She said briefly, "I got them for you for Christmas, but you need them now." How mothers can love!

But summer always came again with the sun, fields of hay, the swimming hole, the picnics, the zoo, and the county fair.

To My Mother

An English teacher once asked her twelfth-grade class to write a story about some person living or dead whom they felt was the greatest person who ever lived. She received some scholarly papers about Franklin Roosevelt, Abraham Lincoln, Winston Churchill, Elizabeth Taylor, Thomas Edison, and others. But Freddie Lowden surprised the class when he read his paper.

"The greatest person who ever lived is my mother."

It would be difficult for any one of us to tell exactly how our mothers molded our lives. We are the product of a mother, a father, brothers and sisters, teachers, friends. We have not only received, but we have given. Our shadow falls on everyone we meet. One writer has said that we like or dislike a person within four seconds after we meet him. Do we dislike a person because he has nothing to contribute to our life? Do we dislike him because he is rude or uninteresting? We like people who are interested in us. Make no mistake here.

Our mother contributed to our life in so many ways. Her relationship with each one of us was not always without trial. We were not always in the mood to be taught. But she loved us and kept trying. It is true that no one can ever take her place. Other people like us if we are nice, but mother took us for better or for worse.

I remember the softness of her bosom as she held my

head close to her and inspected my ears before I went to Sunday school. I remember her bringing me a bowl of potato soup when I was sick in bed with the measles. I remember her baking the big pan of gingerbread that I liked so well. I remember when I was ten years old and she called me to her bedside and told me that she was going away soon, that I was to remember all she had ever tried to teach me and that I was to be good to my father after she was gone. I saw her die a few days later. I know now why some people do not want to die. It is not the fear of death that they have, it is their wanting us who are left behind not to grieve. God takes the hand of those who die and guides them to the land of eternal life. But we who are left behind sometimes must weep in a terrible loneliness.

And then God comes back and he says to us, "You thought I had forgotten you, didn't you? I haven't." And you meet someone who helps you up the hill so that you can see the valley that lies beyond. And you know what it is to grow up and leave behind a childhood world you never wanted to end. God says, "I have work for you to do. Come follow me. I will show you the way. You will never walk alone."

To never walk alone! My mother heard me cry in the night when I was frightened or in pain. My mother tucked me in and kissed me. Now God has taken over. He leads me. Sometimes the way is hard, but though I walk through the valley he leads me beside the still waters. Truly my cup runneth over and I know I shall dwell in his love forever.

The greatest person who ever lived! How God must love us to let us know what a mother is. It was she who taught us to love, to bring joy and peace to the heart.

The Land
of the Stars and Stripes

*But a certain Samaritan, as he journeyed, came where he
was: and when he saw him, he had compassion on him.*

—*Luke 10:33*

As the proud *Queen Elizabeth* swung her bow out of
the harbor of Southampton and slowly and majestically
headed for the English Channel and the Atlantic Ocean
. . . and home, I lifted my eyes from the harbor and the
decks, and I had the thrill that must have come to Francis
Scott Key that early morning when he saw—

> What is that which the breeze, o'er the towering steep,
> As it fitfully blows, half conceals, half discloses . . .
> 'Tis the Star-spangled Banner—O, long may it wave
> O'er the land of the free and the home of the brave.

From the very top of the foremast of the *Queen
Elizabeth* was the Stars and Stripes waving in the Southampton breeze, and below it various other banners of
the sea.

Everywhere I had gone in England I had seen our flag.
It flew side by side with the Union Jack from factory
roofs, store buildings, and in the streets of English cities. I
recalled that all over the country people had said to me,
"You're an American!" It was not a question. It was
spoken with respect and a sort of reverence. The year
was 1947. I asked a good English friend to explain the
flags and he did in a very simple way.

"Suppose that Indiana were surrounded by water.

Suppose all the other forty-seven states had been run over, conquered, and occupied by a ruthless enemy. Then you saw conquest and death staring you in the face. You saw the fires in your bombed cities every night and you helped to carry out the wounded and the dead. We held on for four years knowing that when we died the civilization and culture of Europe would die too.

"Then a great nation, your nation, began to send us money and food and guns and airplanes and men. You rescued our people from death. Believe me, the English meant it when they said, 'We shall never surrender.'" (I am sure they did. In Scotland I rode past mile upon mile of bombs stacked twenty feet high along the highway. Yes, the English would have retreated into the sea to drown before surrender.)

The years have passed. We have had our Dunkirks from time to time, but we are the hope of the world. We are big and we are strong, but no nation fears our conquest. Peace is not bought cheaply because there are those who make money on war. It is not easy to pacify them. But the heartbeat of America is one . . . the desire to see the peoples of the world have hospitals, food, houses, clothing, and education. The past twenty-five years were years of progress. The United States has given its heart and its love and its money to bring a defeated world to life. Sometimes we become too impatient with our government. Sometimes we become too discouraged with other nations. We need to remember that nations like us want respect and dignity and prosperity. It is not always easy to take handouts. Men everywhere want to earn their bread.

Proud we are of our country. We have never asked for anything in return. God has blessed this nation as he did

Abraham. It may well be that he has put upon our shoulders the obligation of being our brother's keeper—but in a sense of helping our brother to help himself. The Stars and Stripes so respected by the world is a symbol of the great American heart.

A Reed
Will Bend

And ye shall know the truth, and the truth shall make you free.

—John 8:32

If you have ever watched a storm sweep over the landscape you have seen great tree limbs snap off and fall to the ground. You have seen the grass bending over. But when the storm has gone and the sun is out, the grass stands tall to the sky. Sometimes men are like trees, sometimes like grass.

Every improvement in the world has come through change. Every generation in the world's history has fought change. The buggy whip manufacturer did not want automobiles because he knew they would put him out of business. There was a time when no woman would appear in church without a hat. Now, where eleven hat shops lined the main street, there is none. The great ocean liners, the *Queen Mary,* the *United States,* and the *Queen Elizabeth* are gone. The airplane spelled their end.

We are living in an age when we can hardly understand the clothes our children wear, their social manner, their hopes and dreams. But we must learn our lesson well, either we shall have to bend or we cannot live in our world.

The church must preach the living Christ, not a Christ of history only. It does not matter too much whether the Bible is taught in the classroom and prayer said. It does matter what kind of teacher stands up in the classroom before our children. The minister used to be at the height of his glory when he expounded for two hours from the pulpit. Today he preaches for fifteen minutes and spends the rest of his time in the hospital, talking to teen-agers, visiting in homes. He is reaching out to those in need in a way that he has never done before.

The most common complaint that I have heard in thirty years in the classroom has been this from the teen-agers, "Our parents won't listen to us." Maybe we have held on too long to the old dictatorship of "you do what I tell you to because I tell you to do it." We have a new generation of young people with questions and ideas. Are we too quick to say no without listening?

Our stores downtown complain of poor business and blame the shopping centers. They have kept the same hours from nine to five for fifty years. They will not bend. Mothers work today. A great percentage of our population works until four or five o'clock. And to shop—the people go where the stores are open.

This is not to paint a dark picture, but to make us aware of change and the need for us to be openminded and willing to bend if it means a better world in which to live. Thanks to the men and women, the designers, the workers who have given us beautiful homes today, luxury cars, a great variety of food for our tables, color in our clothes, and new styles that we thought shocking only a few years ago. How wonderful it was that some man dreamed up a thermostat for automatic heat, even if it did mean putting out of business the companies that made coal shovels. And how marvelous the thousands upon thousands of paperbacks that bring reading to our people at a reasonable price.

It seems that one of the traits of the people of this nation has been progress, and this has meant change. A few have dared to step ahead. And the result has been a better land in which to live. Do not live with a closed mind, but continue to learn and to thrill every day you live.

There Is Music
Wherever You Go

These things have I spoken unto you, that my joy might remain in you, and that your joy might be full.

—John 15:11

The Austrian Alps near the abbey in Salzburg are among the most beautiful places in the world. The blue lakes and the green meadows and, of course, the haunting strains of music from the heart of Julie Andrews: "the hills are alive with the sound of music." One summer day I looked at these beautiful Alps for the last time, trying to drink into my mind this scene that it might last forever.

As this book, *Joy Begins with You,* comes to an end, I think here in the glowing twilight of the years since childhood, of the people who have touched my life. So it is with you. We can never be alone in this life. We have only to close our eyes and recall the great men and women who have touched our lives, passed on, but left within our lives the sound of music.

Alma was one of these. I heard a girl say once, "Oh, I just can't have my party Friday night if you can't come. Can you come if I have it Saturday?" We watch other people. We copy them. We try to adopt what we like about them. We have the spirit of God in our lives that calls us ever to climb and to grow and to be. And so sometimes a tear comes into our eyes, and the heart becomes very warm as we sit and think of the moments in our life when we have walked on the mountaintop.

The blue ribbon we won on our prize pig, the honor sweater for football, the man-of-the-year award by a service club, the announcement from a nurse "you have a new baby boy," the letter from the dean "your son has made the Dean's list in college," the warm evening under the stars surrounded by lace and perfume and the words "I love you," the pride when a son speaks "I want you to meet my father," the warmth of "without you I never could have done it," the note "thank you for just being you," the boat trip up the Hudson River, the hours you spent in finding just the right book, the telephone call to take me to the doctor, the flower that came to the hospital room, the surprise birthday dinner, the invitation to use your swimming pool, the sharing of your heart and your love in a thousand ways—how can I name them all?

When Jesus said to Peter, "Feed my sheep," he was not asking the impossible. When he said, "take my yoke upon your shoulder," he meant, "You'll never walk alone." You have a partnership with God. You have taken the key to heaven when you help another. "The Sound of Music," as a movie, captivated the world because it was filled with love and caring. When we care for others our lives are filled with light. It was truly said about someone I knew, "Wherever she goes there is music."

I thought, as I walked down the mountainside from the green meadow near Salzburg, Austria, to meet my train for Zurich, Switzerland, that there would be no music in the hills had God not first planted music deep in the heart of us.